The *Quick* Wise Guide to Writing Grant Proposals

HOW TO WRITE
A PERSUASIVE PROPOSAL

Waddy Thompson

Stitch-in-Time Books

Copyright © 2017, Waddy Thompson

All rights reserved. No part of this book shall be reproduced, stored in a retrieval system, or transmitted by any means, electronic, mechanical, photocopying, recording, or otherwise, without written permission from the publisher. No patent liability is assumed with respect to the use of the information contained herein. Although every precaution has been taken in the preparation of this book, the publisher and author assume no responsibility for errors or omissions. Neither is any liability assumed for damages resulting from the use of information contained herein.

Note: This publication contains the opinions and ideas of its author. It is intended to provide helpful and informative material on the subject matter covered. It is sold with the understanding that the author and publisher are not engaged in rendering professional services in the book. If the reader requires personal assistance or advice, a competent professional should be consulted.

The author specifically disclaims any responsibility for any liability, loss, or risk, personal or otherwise, which is incurred as a consequence, directly or indirectly, of the use and application of any of the contents of this book.

All nonprofits described in examples in this book are fictitious and any resemblance to any actual nonprofit is coincidental.

The Quick Wise Guide to Writing Grant Proposals
Waddy Thompson
1st Edition, November 2017
Stitch-in-Time Books, Sarasota, Florida, U.S.A.

ISBN: 978-0-9985124-4-0

www.grantadviser.com

Cover concept by Flyleaf Creative; design by Jakob Vala
Copyediting by Jill Gallagher
Images used under license from Shutterstock.com

Contents

Introduction 1

Articulate the Problem 4

Present Your Credentials 8

    Dealing with the Competition 9

    Testimonials 11

    Pulling It All Together 12

How You Will Fix the Problem 15

    Purpose of the Program 16

    How You Will Make It Happen 17

    Who Will Do What 20

    When and Where 21

    Who Will Benefit 23

    Looking Inward; Looking Outward 25

    How You Will Know You Have Done Well 26

    Summing It All Up 31

Some Notes About Tone and Style 34

    Strive for a Conversational Tone 35

    Final Notes 36

Sample Grant Proposal Narrative 38

About the Author 46

Introduction

The grant-seeking process can cover several months, encompassing researching and contacting potential funders; interviewing staff who will carry out the project; collecting staff bios, financial reports, and other supporting materials; and developing a budget.[1]

With so many things to do, the actual writing of a persuasive narrative description of your project can get shortchanged. That's why I have written this short guide: to focus on helping you improve your writing and organizational skills so that you can create a convincing narrative that tells your story and wins grants.

The narrative (also referred to as the proposal) is equally important no matter what type of funder you are approaching: foundations, corporations, government agencies, or even individuals.

A good narrative presents the case for support by immediately capturing the reader's imagination. It goes on to describe the problem you plan to solve, how your charity will work to solve it, and your qual-

---

[1] If you would like to learn about the different types of funders, researching funders, organizing your grant-seeking efforts, developing convincing budgets, and freelance grant writing, take a look at my comprehensive book on the subject, *The Wise Guide to Winning Grants* (Stitch-in-Time Books, 2017), which is available in paperback and in all e-book formats. (This book is a considerable expansion of that book's Chapter 13.)

ifications for doing this work. It must also convey a feeling of urgency to make the reader want to give you the grant right now. The case for support is the essential part of any funding request.

Good cases for support bear a strong relationship to other types of persuasive writing. In their book *Made to Stick: Why Some Ideas Survive and Others Die*, Chip Heath and Dan Heath sum up the elements of successful writing with the mnemonic "SUCCES," which stands for "simple, unexpected, concrete, credible, emotional, and stories." That's the best summary of how to create good fundraising copy I've ever seen. As you read on, think about how each part of the narrative fulfills one or more aspects of the "SUCCES" principle.

I recommend following a simple three-part structure for organizing most proposals:

1. Articulate the Problem: What problem or issue do you seek to address? Your funder will most likely know something (or possibly a lot) about the issue, but be clear about how you see the problem.

2. Present Your Credentials: Why are you the right nonprofit to carry out this program? Have you conducted similar programs in the past? What experience does the leadership of your organization contribute to your ability to carry out the program? What endorsements do you have?

3. Describe How You Will Fix the Problem: This is where you get into

the details about what you plan to do. You will also demonstrate how organized your thinking is and how well you understand the issue.

The following chapters will help you convincingly describe your program, putting you well on your way to receiving funding. At the end of the book is a sample of a complete proposal narrative, as well as a reference to where you can find other helpful samples.

CHAPTER 1

Articulate the Problem

This chapter is about how to define the need you seek to meet, but first thing's first: Start your proposal with a single sentence that makes a request for a specific amount of money and states what you will do with the grant. Here's an example:

> *The Neighborhood Music School seeks a $50,000 grant from the Smith and Jones Foundation to bring after-school music instruction to children living in the city's homeless shelters.*

Short, concise, direct: It prepares the reader for what's to come. You'd be surprised at how many proposals are submitted without a specific request for money. Foundation trustees aren't mind readers, so get this out of the way at the very beginning of your narrative.

The first step in making the case for support is clearly demonstrating that a problem exists and that you thoroughly understand it. So what problem are you trying to solve? Feeding the hungry, housing the homeless, educating children, training people for new jobs, healing the sick, making a film, and bringing the arts to underserved communities are a few examples of issues nonprofits address.

Following your request for a grant, a great way to capture the reader's attention is with an astonishing fact that demonstrates the depth of the problem. Consider this statement from a charity that provides education to people in refugee camps:

The average time someone spends in a refugee camp is 17 years.

That shocked me the first time I heard it. It made me want to immediately get out my checkbook. Seventeen years means that children spend their *entire childhood* as refugees, so the need for education as a pathway out of the camps is obviously important and deserving of support.

A nonprofit that provides meals for homeless families might use:

Nine percent of the children in our city go to bed hungry every night.

Again, you immediately see a need, feel an emotional response, and want to help.

The important thing is for your eye-catching opening to be meaningful *to your reader*. "George Inness has not been the subject of a major New York museum exhibition in more than 20 years" doesn't produce quite the heart-tugs of the previous two examples, but if you did your research correctly, the person reading your proposal will care enough about American Impressionist painter George Innes to be moved by that statement and want to take action.

You might also start with an eye-catching statistic about your nonprofit. Something like:

> *More than 18,500 seniors in our community receive their main meal of the day from Senior Care.*

The scope of what Senior Care is already doing is impressive and the large number shows the enormity of seniors' needs. Statistics help you demonstrate a need for a program, but be sure you can back them up. Also, don't use national statistics for a local issue; if the number of homeless youth in your community is the need you're trying to address, the number nationwide won't help your cause.

You can make your need statement stronger by including statements from neutral third parties that express or reinforce the need you seek to address. These could be stories in the press or studies that other groups have done, including studies commissioned by funders. This not only reinforces the need for your program, it also shows that your organization sees itself as part of the larger issue and that it keeps abreast of the latest thought on and activity related to a subject. Here are a couple of examples:

> *The Daily Times reported that Mayor Thomas stated in his speech to the Rotary Club last week that "hunger remains one of the city's most pressing problems, especially among the transient population that lives on the fringes of the industrial area." Community Food Bank agrees,*

> which is why we approach the distribution of meals through a mobile facility rather than depending on our main office to handle all clients.

Or:

> Social Think Tank, Inc., in its report issued last month, drew attention to the difficulty that traditional place-based food banks have in reaching the neediest populations, which tend to exist outside the central urban areas where most of these agencies are located. Community Food Bank agrees, which is why we approach the distribution of meals through a mobile facility rather than depending on our main office to handle all clients.

Establishing the need comes first in the proposal, because if you can't convince the reader that there is a genuine need, the rest is irrelevant.

Chapter 2

Present Your Credentials[2]

Now that you've convinced the reader that there is a need that must be addressed, you have to persuade her that your nonprofit is qualified to deal with the problem. Questions a funder will be thinking about include:

- What is the nonprofit's experience working on this issue?

- How long has it worked on this or similar issues?

- What success has it had in the past?

---

[2] In some cases, this section might work better as the third section if an understanding of your qualifications cannot be conveyed without getting heavily into a description of your program.

- What professional expertise does it bring to addressing the problem? Is it a recognized authority on this topic?

- Are there other nonprofits working on this issue, some of which the funder might already be supporting?

Let's look at these questions, starting with the last one.

Dealing with the Competition

It's quite likely that the funder has made a grant to an organization similar to yours in the past. That's probably one of the reasons you decided to write to them. The funder will therefore want to know how what you propose to do fits in with what others are doing. Is your approach different or complementary? Why is what you propose to do needed if others are working on the same issue? If no one else is dealing with the issue, is there a reason for that?

Never trash the competition in your proposal. Today's competitor is tomorrow's panelist deciding the fate of your grant proposal. It's also not polite or necessary. That's not to say you shouldn't contrast your approach to that of other organizations, but you should do so in a way that offends no one. For example, you could write:

The Community Food Bank provides meals to 1,200 people daily who aren't currently served by other social service providers.

Or:

> *The Community Food Bank provides meals to 1,200 people daily who are unable to get transportation to food services offered by other social service providers.*

Or:

> *The Community Food Bank's work complements that of similar nonprofits in our area by seeking out people whose irregular work hours, housing location, or immigration status makes it less likely that they will take advantage of existing services.*

All of those are much more positive than "The Community Food Bank provides meals to 1,200 people daily who Food for People does not reach because of its unwillingness to look outside its immediate neighborhood."

Consider the following three statements. They state the same facts, yet the third creates a totally different (and negative) impression of the nonprofit asking for the grant.

Hometown Health Service's mobile unit provides daily diagnostic testing and diabetes treatment for 100 people who do not currently have regular access to free health services.

Hometown Health Service's mobile unit provides daily diagnostic testing and diabetes treatment for 100 people who lack transportation to the county's existing low-cost or free clinics.

Tri-County Health Center's mobile unit provides daily diagnostic testing and diabetes treatment for 100 people who are not served by Hilltown Medical Center and other facilities that treat only people who are able to come to their facility and can afford a minimum fee.

Hometown Health Service found two ways to emphasize its unique service (it goes where no other providers go) without denigrating other services, as Tri-County Health Center did.

Testimonials

Testimonials from clients about your charity's ability to carry out a project will also strengthen your case for support. A quote praising your work from an acknowledged expert in your field adds credibility, but an emotional quote from a grateful client will be remembered long after statistics have been forgotten.

When quoting individuals in a proposal, it's not necessary to use scholarly conventions to indicate minor changes. After all, people will usually appreciate your making them sound more articulate than they are – as long as you don't change the meaning of their words. Indicating each place you've made minor changes will only make for awkward reading and might even make the person quoted look bad. If you're uncomfortable making changes, you can always show the revised quote to the person quoted for approval. Here's what I mean:

Original client statement:

> *The Health Service gave my Bonnie, who had broken her toe, and me compassionate and expert care late last Thursday night. And they gave it right when it was needed.*

Here's a more readable attribution:

> *The staff at Community Health Services provided my family with compassionate and expert care right when it was needed.*

The changes certainly did not distort what the client said in any way, but present it in a manner that is easier to read and grammatically correct.

Pulling It All Together

Funders want to invest in successful nonprofits, so your track record is important. Get specific about your nonprofit's qualifications: Has it been recognized with any awards? How long has your organization existed? How long has it worked in this program area? How many people work for you? What are your sources of funding? In short, present a succinct picture of the resources you can bring to this issue.

The Community Food Bank might present its case for support in a statement like this:

> *Since 1987, The Community Food Bank (CFB) has helped feed our city's least fortunate citizens. It has provided more than 95,000 meals to 6,500 people since its founding. Its 119 employees now produce and serve 2,400 meals daily.*
>
> *CFB's mobile facilities (its food trucks) are the primary reason it has reached so many people. CFB has taken hot breakfasts to areas where day laborers wait for work*

and parked outside factories to serve lunch to employees who work for less than the minimum wage. CFB food trucks also spend hours feeding entire families each weekend in the city's poorest neighborhoods. "I am so grateful for CFB's help in feeding my family. When I see your big yellow truck in the neighborhood, I know that my family will eat well that day," said a Chelsea mother.

Meals are also served at our central facility, but CFB is unique in local service providers in the people who are served in their places of work or residence (60%). No one needs to give identification or any type of credential to receive a free meal. The Rotary Club has recognized CFB's work to alleviate hunger with its Nonprofit Leader of the Year award three times, in 1992, 1999, and 2015, most recently citing the organization's "unwavering dedication to those most in need."

A quote from a grateful client and mention of a civic award add emotion and credibility, and the statistics at the beginning demonstrate the nonprofit's long and successful experience alleviating hunger in the community. It also highlights its unique strategy for addressing hunger (the food trucks) without denigrating any other charity working in this field.

A nonprofit that does not have a substantial track record but does have highly qualified individuals working for it might present its qualifications something like this:

The Neighborhood Music School has hired James Smith to organize and work directly with the children living in shelters for homeless families. Mr. Smith has more than fifteen years' experience working with children from underprivileged backgrounds. He has the unique academic qualifications of master's degrees in both music education and social work. He was one of three recipients of the Maryville Chamber of Commerce 2011 Citizen of the Year award for a similar project he ran in public schools for three years.

Mr. Smith's specific experience, combined with the Music School's 65-year history as a music education provider in the community, well prepares us to carry out this program.

Don't be afraid to brag a little to inspire confidence in your ability to carry out the proposed program.

CHAPTER 3

How You Will Fix the Problem

Now we will address the central part of the proposal: What will you do to fix the problem?

- What resources will you call upon? (This includes experience and knowledge, personnel, facilities (such as a clinic space or classrooms), and fiscal resources, including money from other sources than the grant for which you're applying.)

- How will you demonstrate your success at the end of the grant period?

- Will your successful completion of your proposed project make short- or long-term differences?

That's a lot to cover, so let's break it down into sections.

Purpose of the Program

You should always create a one-sentence summary that describes the project's essence in a way that makes a strong case for funding. And it should be a *really good sentence*! If you can't do that, you don't understand the project well enough to write the proposal. Review your notes and talk again with people involved in the program until you can write one dynamite sentence.

A strong, even bold, statement of purpose at the beginning of this section grabs the reader's attention and sets an ambitious tone for the rest of the proposal. For example:

> *Community Food Bank will daily relieve the hunger of 2,400 homeless people, none of whom are now reached by any other agency.* ["Relieve the hunger" is more moving than "feed."]

> *Nonprofit managers attending the Managing Your Board workshops will come away with the knowledge and skills to transform their relationships with their boards, resulting in more productive nonprofits throughout the city.* ["Transform" is more inspiring than "change."]

> *People living in refugee camps will find their way to resettlement through the education we provide, making them self-supporting and valuable members of the local economy.* [The second half of the sentence illustrates the long-term benefits of the program.]

> *Our City's forgotten children will find solace and an outlet for self-expression through the Neighborhood Music School's out-*

reach program. ["Forgotten children," "solace," and "self-expression" are all weighted with emotion.]

You can use your moving summary statement at the beginning of your proposal along with your specific grant request or as an opening for your cover letter.

Note that in each of the examples above, I used the helper verb *will* instead of *would*. *Will* makes a more positive statement, implying that the project will go forward no matter what. *Would* is weaker, implying that the project is not only conditional on this grant coming through, but perhaps on other factors as well.

Beginning grant writers often hesitate to make bold, sweeping statements, having been taught in English classes to avoid generalizations and unsubstantiated statements. Sweeping statements are a means of getting the reader's attention, and although you need to support your assertions with evidence, the substantiation doesn't necessarily have to immediately follow your bold declaration.

How You Will Make It Happen

You have to give the funder a concrete description of how the program will work. Be as specific as possible without getting so specific that you limit the flexibility of your program staff to respond to current needs. Will you meet with each client five or six times? How many hot lunches will you distribute? What are the steps your literacy program follows to involve adults and children? These are the kinds of details you must include. Let's look at a couple of short examples:

Managing Your Board: *The Managing Your Board workshop series will consist of four weekly two-hour sessions attended by 14-20 nonprofit leaders. Workshops will begin with a lecture by an expert in board and executive director issues followed by a question-and-answer period. The themes of the workshops will be Avoiding Micromanagement, Helping a Board Fundraise, Making the Executive Director's Performance Review Work for You, and Building the Board You Need. During the final half hour of each session, participants will break down into groups of ten or fewer to discuss what they have learned in practical terms that relate to their organizations.*

Music for Kids: *The Music for Kids program will provide musical instruction at the local Leopard's Club to young people living in the city's largest homeless shelter. Transportation will be provided to the Leopard's Club after school two days each week. These children remain a transient population requiring short-term goals that can be met in a limited time. Therefore, the emphasis will be on learning rhythm and simple songs rather than learning to read music. Most of the 90-minute sessions will be devoted to working together, but there will also be time set aside during each session for more personalized attention from the seven teaching assistants.*

Note that both paragraphs briefly describe the format of the sessions, give information on the content, and give the time participants will be involved in the programs. A real proposal would go into additional details. For the board workshops, that might include the types of nonprofit taking part and descriptions of each session. For the music program, this might include more background on the children and how the alliance between the music school and the Leopard's Club came about.

Take your audience into consideration when deciding how technical you can be in your proposal. You want to give details and examples the reader will understand. In general, proposals reviewed by peer panels can include more technical language than ones that will be seen only by foundation trustees who may or may not possess technical knowledge related to your proposal. (Also see my comments on the use of jargon in Chapter 4.)

Do not mention anyone or any organization as partnering with you without clearing it with them first. This is especially true if a peer panel will evaluate your proposal—someone on the panel might know your desired partner. Keep in mind who might be deciding the fate of your proposal. Be especially sure you don't criticize any other organization.

Specifying the financial resources you will commit to the program reassures the funder that you have the means to carry out the program. Beyond this grant, you can fund the program with money raised specifically for a program, or you can allocate money from your operating funds to help cover program expenses. Both sources demonstrate your commitment to the program, and a mixture of the two will present the greatest level of program stability. You should mention any funds already raised for the program beyond the immediate period to show the funder that the program is viable for the long term.

Who Will Do What

The funder will also want to know who will carry out the program. Will your staff do everything, or will you use outside consultants? It's critical that the staffing described in this section exactly matches the staffing detailed in your program budget. You needn't get too specific, but give them an idea of where the responsibilities will lie.

The staffing sections of the two programs described previously might read like this:

> Managing Your Board: *The director of programs will select the consultants who will lead the workshops in consultation with other members of the program staff and from referrals from colleagues at other service organizations. Program staff will manage enrollment and be present at each workshop to assist with breakout groups. One consultant will lead each of the first three workshops, with two consultants jointly leading the final session.*
>
> Music for Kids: *Our outreach program will be led by consultant James Smith, a leader in community outreach programs. He will train and work with our education staff to provide musical instruction to the children. His work will be supervised by the director of programs, who will review progress with Mr. Smith and the instructors weekly. We will pay a small fee to our partner organization for the use of their bus and bus driver to transport children from schools to the program space. We will also pay the custodial staff at the partner facility from program funds, although the Leopard's Club is donating the space.*

Note that in the first example, the people leading the workshops have not yet been chosen, whereas in the second one, the principle person is specified. It's always better to show that you've pinned down the important people taking part in your project, but sometimes the selection of those people will be part of your program process.

When and Where

Foundations typically make grants for a one-year period, although there can be exceptions. If you expect to need more than a year to complete your project, check to see if the funder permits a longer time period; if so, ask for the extra time.

Funders frequently ask for a timeline of significant events in the project. In most cases, nothing should appear in your timeline outside of the grant period unless specifically labeled as such. Here's a sample timeline for the music for kids program taking place in school year 2018-2019:

July-August 2018	Meet with social workers at several homeless shelters to determine feasibility of working together. Review anticipated participation numbers with facility operators.
September 10-28, 2018	Visit shelters during after-school hours to meet with parents and enroll children. Set busing schedule for children from each shelter.

October 1-December 14, 2018	Hold weekly sessions, Mondays-Thursdays, two days for each shelter. Follow up as needed with shelter staff and parents for children missing sessions and new children eligible to join the program.
December 17-20, 2018	Review reports and analyze effectiveness of individual sites and overall program. Write interim report to funders for January submission.
January 7-June 14, 2019	Hold weekly sessions, Mondays-Thursdays, two days for each shelter. Follow up as needed with shelter staff and parents for children missing sessions and new children eligible to join the program.
June 17-28, 2019	Review reports and analyze effectiveness of individual sites and overall program. Prepare final report for partners and funders.

You will also want to be specific about where program activities will take place. Will you use your own facilities? Rent outside facilities? Will a partner organization provide free space? In the case of the music program, the Leopard's Club is providing free space. You will want to describe that space's location, size, capacity, and amenities.

Who Will Benefit

Who will benefit from the program is, of course, *the* important part of a program description. Foundations and other funders seek to solve a social problem. In submitting a proposal, you are volunteering to help them solve that problem. Focusing on the needs of the ultimate beneficiaries of the program (rather than on your charity) will resonate most strongly with the funder's interests.

Emotional stories about the people your project serves enrich this section. Even a short anecdote gives your proposal a human dimension the reader can respond to compassionately. Here's an example from the program to educate people in refugee camps:

The average time someone spends in a refugee camp is 17 years, and for Maya, that time started when she was only 13 years old. Her escape from her war-torn country took her through many harrowing experiences, but eventually, she and her family found refuge in a large camp located in Jordan. With her parents concentrating on keeping their six children together, safe, and healthy, education was largely ignored. But Maya had always loved school and learning, and she pushed her parents to find an outlet for her passion.

Fortunately, their camp was run in partnership with the Refugee Education Agency (REA), which provides classes at high school level through two years of college. The years went by slowly for Maya's family, but Maya excelled in the refugee school as she had back home. When she was nineteen, she used her education to get a bookkeeping job with the camp administration, which led to a similar job in the local community. With her means of earning a living established, she was able to find a home for her entire family in a nearby town, and today they all live safe, productive lives there.

Maya's story is but one of hundreds of successful stories from our program. The U.N. High Commission on Refugees has praised the REA's work in this and in other camps. With additional funding, we can help even more inspiring young people, freeing them and their families from the unstable, poverty-stricken lives of refugee camps.

Notice that this story fulfills all of the Heath brothers' criteria for persuasive writing mentioned in the Introduction: it is Simple, it begins with something Unexpected, it is specific and Concrete, the mention of the U.N. agency makes it Credible, it's Emotional, and, of course, it is in the form of a Story.

This section of the narrative must also include some cold, hard facts (metrics) about how many people you will serve. Numbers can make a huge difference in judging the worthiness of your proposal. Giving exact numbers before the program even begins might be impractical, but you can give ranges.

You might feel you need to inflate the number of people who will be served to make the funder feel like it will be getting its money's worth. Don't! Those numbers will come back to haunt you when it's time to report on your results. But don't give numbers that are too low either, or funders might think the program isn't cost effective.

Funders realize that different kinds of projects are more efficient than others and that efficiency is not the sole criteria for worthiness. A website might cost $50,000 to make and reach 250,000 people (20 cents per person), whereas a workshop series might cost $50,000 and serve 100 people ($500 per person) but in a much more direct and personal way than the website. The value of the program is not just in the math—it's in the ability of your organization to deliver a program that accomplishes its goals and serves a worthy purpose.

Looking Inward; Looking Outward

The program you propose to carry out should align with your charity's mission. Explain how this program fits in with everything else you do.

> *Hometown Health Service has been dedicated to helping people with diabetes since its founding in 1982. Believing that early detection is critical to future treatment, it has developed a range of programs to encourage testing. Its new mobile unit makes it easier for people who lack personal transportation or work long or irregular hours to receive testing.*

Proposals that are too inward looking—that is, concentrated too much on what your organization needs—are doomed to failure in most cases. For example, you would never include the following in a program grant proposal:

> *Hometown Health Service seeks funding to close a budget gap that threatens its services.*

That statement makes it sound as if you haven't been doing your job to raise funds and to balance income and expenses. The funder might think that giving you a grant would be a bad investment.

Proposals that focus on clients' needs — the people you will help — stand a much better chance of success. *Remember: funders make grants to solve a problem other than helping you make your budget goal.*

Even a grant proposal to improve the technology at your charity should include information about how the charity's clients will benefit. For example, rather than writing about how the new equipment will make life easier for your employees, you might write:

By upgrading to the latest software and bringing in a high-speed internet connection, case workers will be able to assist 30% more clients every day in finding affordable healthcare.

The benefit of the technology is shown directly affecting your agency's clients, the very ones the funder wants to help.

How You Will Know You Have Done Well

Program evaluation should be an integral part of everything your charity does. How else will you be able to show others that you have done the job well, that people will benefit enough to justify the expense, and that the program should continue? A lot of organizations coast along with only anecdotal evidence of program success, eventually getting an unwelcome surprise when a funder starts asking hard questions, leading to the possible loss of funding.

The importance of program evaluation is one of the most dramatic changes I have seen in the nonprofit world during my thirty-five years in the business. In olden days, you wrote a nice letter to the funder telling them how well everything went and thanking them for making it possible, and you were done. Not so today.

With the enormous increase in the number of nonprofits and the consequent increase in competition for funds, funders of all kinds now insist that charities measure the effectiveness of their programs and include in their grant requests how they will evaluate what they have done. Foundations want their investment in your charity to be money well spent. Additionally, corporate and government funders must justify their grant programs to their stockholders or to the elected representatives who determine their budgets, respectively.

Don't try to hide a lack of evaluative procedures by giving some vague statement like "Our charity follows a rigorous evaluative process to assess the efficacy of all programs through surveys, interviews with participants, focus groups, and independent evaluators." That's all well and good, but how will you evaluate *this* program? A sound evaluation provides excellent material for all future proposals.

In the next chapter, I admonish you to avoid jargon, but evaluation is one place where you must know and use the right lingo. Here are a few of the most important terms you will need:

Formative Methods: This is fancy-talk for observing how a program is progressing while it is taking place, focusing on the process. Perhaps you have stood in the back of a class noting students' reactions to the teacher's presentation. You always thought you were just taking notes, but you were actually employing formative evaluation methods!

Summative Methods: When the project is complete and you do a survey, formal or informal, of participants or of those who ran the program, you are using summative methods to measure the outcomes. In other words, you are summing up the experience.

Next come the all-important goals, objectives, benchmarks, and strategies. Goals and objectives are often spoken about as if they are the same thing, but they're quite different.

Goals represent the ultimate achievement of your program or organization; they might well be so great as to be unreachable or realized long after the grant period.

Objectives are the measurable steps you need to take to get there. You will usually need to accomplish several objectives to reach the goal.

Remember:

- Goals are broad; objectives are narrow.
- Goals are general intentions; objectives are precise.
- Goals are intangible; objectives are tangible.
- Goals are abstract; objectives are concrete.
- Goals can't be validated as is; objectives can be validated.

Benchmarks are measures you must reach along the way to accomplish each objective.

Strategies are the activities you will undertake to reach each benchmark.

Here are two examples:

> The United Nations: *The ultimate goal of the United Nations might be thought of as world peace. Its objectives embrace universal education and health care and elimination of nuclear armaments. The benchmarks to be achieved would include resolving specific disputes around the world and improving agri-*

culture and education worldwide. Strategies would be holding peace talks, delivering food to impoverished people, and establishing better health care and education facilities.

Children's Literacy Program: *The goal of a children's literacy program might be to have every child in a school reading at grade level by the end of third grade. An objective for a one-year grant for this program might be that kindergarten and first-grade students will read at grade level or above by the end of the first year. Benchmarks that must be achieved to reach that objective would be for all K-3 students to be enrolled in the program, and for students to meet with the specialist teachers for an hour, three times each week. A strategy would be to hire specialist teachers to conduct the program.*

You can see from these two examples (one global and one local) that the goals and objectives are kind of common sense, but if you get the terms muddled, you will come off looking inept and be much less likely to receive a grant.

For the workshop series on How to Manage Your Board described earlier, an evaluation plan might read like this:

Short surveys in which participants will be asked to grade the speaker, the content, and the overall workshop on a five-point scale will be provided at the end of each session. They will also be asked for information about themselves and the organizations for which they work so that cross-tab reports can be prepared to assess the program from many angles; for example, comparing the responses of representatives from social service organizations to those from educational ones. We will also interview workshop leaders to gain insights from their point of view. Subsequent workshop series will be modified should the analysis of this data indicate a need for a different approach or different instructors. The cross-tab reports will also help focus the marketing and outreach for future programs.

Given the young ages of the participants in the music workshops for homeless children, surveys would not be as effective a method of evaluation. In this case, an evaluation from the charity's program director might be best, especially if you can show that she has a background that allows her to complete the evaluation objectively.

The program director will compile and analyze weekly reports from the program consultant and instructors based on her twenty-five years of experience. She will also interview each of them to determine what aspects of the program worked best and if there are any children requiring special attention. Her resulting report will be used to adjust the current programs and to modify the program in future years.

Your evaluation methods, as well as your specific goals and objectives, form an integral part of any grant proposal. Careful preparation of the evaluation section of your proposal accomplishes two things:

(1) It makes your proposal stronger.

(2) It makes it much easier to report on your project. With established objectives, benchmarks, and strategies, your report will have substance and clarity.

One final note: Staff members can certainly perform the evaluation, but an evaluation completed by an outsider is even more valuable. There are many consultants who do this work. They can be quite expensive, but their costs can sometimes be included as part of your grant budget. One foundation I worked with was willing to add

$30,000 to its usual $80,000 grant to pay for an independent evaluator.

Summing It All Up

At the end of your proposal, clearly sum it all up for the reader. The summary should usually be no more than one or two short paragraphs and should include:

- A moving argument for funding your proposal (which includes both needs and the intended results), stated differently from elsewhere in the proposal.

- A request for the specific amount of the grant you're seeking. (A repeat from the beginning, but necessary.)

- A brief account of how you will sustain the program beyond the current grant request.

- A thank you for considering your proposal.

This is where you want the reader to hear the violins soar and see the cowboy ride off into the sunset. *This is your big ending.* Make it a good one. Here's an example for the Music for Kids program:

Life in a shelter for homeless families is especially hard on the children. Going to school provides some respite, but often the school day simply exchanges one institutional environment for another. Music for Kids will ensure that for at least three hours each week, as many as sixty children living in shelters will be taken out of the institutional environment and out of themselves through music.

Individual and small group instruction will provide much-needed personal attention, and group singing will encourage community and cooperation. Such simple activities have an enormous potential to assist these young people, as the recent study by Urban Educators Conference shows.

The $20,000 grant we have requested will provide 33% of the $60,000 in funding for this program. We have $25,000 already committed from the Community Foundation, which has supported this program for six years. We seek a $25,000 grant to match the Community Foundation. The balance will come from individual donations allocated for this program. Continuity in this program is important for the children we serve, and our development staff continually research potential new foundation and individual funders.

Thank you for considering our grant request. It will make a wonderful music program possible for these lost citizens of our city.

The issue of sustainability is a tricky one: You no doubt hope the funder will support your program for several years at least, but you have to show that you are prepared to find other funders to take over in the event they cannot offer sustained support.

A common question is "How long should the proposal be?" Without being facetious, the answer is "As long as it needs to be." Some funders impose limits on length (as little as three pages), but I've written fifteen-page proposals that didn't seem long, considering the complexity of the programs.

The important thing is to stay focused on the project and avoid any tangents. If the proposal will be more than five pages, you might want to include a table of contents, and you'll definitely want section headers to help readers skim through to find particular information in a proposal of any length.

Nothing in the project description should deviate from the sole purpose of generating interest and enthusiasm for the project. Don't get sidetracked recounting your charity's history or describing other programs.

Avoid the curse of too much knowledge. You're an expert on the issue your proposal seeks to address. That's all well and good, but don't think you have to include everything you know about the issue in any one program narrative. Stay on track, and don't let your writing drift off into unessential information.

Chapter 4

Some Notes About Tone and Style

When you are writing, just as when you are speaking, remember your audience. And by "audience," I don't just mean the program officer who will first read your proposal or the peer panel that may review it – I mean everyone who will read it.

Program officers' and peer panelists' knowledge of the subject of your proposal may well be similar to or greater than your own, but foundation trustees will also see at least part of your proposal, and they are the ones who will make the final decision on funding. Also, my guess is that if you use plain language in your proposal, the program officer's summary is likely to be clearer than if you indulged in a paroxysm of jargon meant to impress them with your erudition, thus obfuscating the meaning of your primary thesis. (See what I mean?)

In fact, you should always try to avoid jargon, with the one exception noted in the previous chapter. That includes your nonprofit's jargon, jargon common to your field, and jargon used by funders. Jargon is really just a form of slang, with no place in a reasoned argument to fund your organization. And think about it: One reason people use jargon is to show that they are part of the "in crowd," which means that anyone who doesn't understand the term-du-jour is part of the "out crowd." Do you want to risk making a foundation trustee think they are part of the "out crowd?"

"But," you might well ask, "what about the jargon used by the funders themselves?" Granted, some funders write their guidelines in the kind of prose that requires a thesaurus (or insider's knowledge) to interpret. If you parrot that language back to them, you've proven only that you read the guidelines – not that you understood them.

I'm not suggesting that you dumb-down the proposal or define every technical term. What I do recommend is that you write your proposals at a level that both shows respect for your audience and demonstrates your ability to communicate your nonprofit's case to a lay audience. The experts will be impressed, not put off, by your ability to explain complex issues in simple terms. The lawyer portrayed by Denzel Washington in the movie *Philadelphia* was fond of saying something like, "Explain it to me like I'm a six-year-old." You don't have to go that far, but it's a good principle to keep in mind.

Strive for a Conversational Tone

Keeping a conversational tone is one of the most important things I teach writers. Why? A conversational tone automatically eliminates long, winding sentences and excessive jargon. You don't speak that way, so there's no reason to write that way. Just as importantly, a conversational tone helps establish the all-important personal contact with the reader. Grants are made by individuals, not faceless institutions, and connecting person-to-person is critical in making a persuasive case for funding.

To develop a conversational tone, have a non-expert read your proposal and point out anything he had to read twice or that broke the flow. Even better – read the entire proposal aloud yourself. Can't finish a sentence in one breath? Then it's too long. Find your tongue tripping over a phrase? Rewrite it. The acid test is to read your proposal aloud to a friend outside the profession. I'll bet that your friend's facial expressions alone will tell you when you've lapsed into jargon or awkward writing.

If you can keep it simple and personable, you will separate your proposal from the many, many others and increase your chances for success. I heartily recommend one of the very best works on writing well: William Strunk Jr. and E.B. White's *The Elements of Style*. Although originally published decades ago, there is no better guide to clear writing and none more enjoyable to read.

Final Notes

Organizing your proposal as I've outlined in this book will ensure that everything required is included and presented in a logical order. But keep in mind that the order in which you present the information can vary, especially if a funder specifies some other order. Always follow the funder's instructions to the letter. Proposals that don't follow instructions are often tossed out without any consideration.

Before you submit a proposal, be sure to let someone directly involved in the program read it to be sure nothing got lost in the translation, so to speak.

And remember:

- If you can't sum up a project in one persuasive sentence, you don't understand it well enough to write a proposal.

- Making a clear case for supporting your charity includes information on what problems you seek to solve, how you will solve them, who will work on the project, and most importantly, who will benefit from it.

- Proposals that focus on your clients' or constituents' needs are stronger than those that stress the needs of your nonprofit.

- Take into consideration who will be reading your proposal when deciding how technical you can be.

- Use concrete program evaluative methods you are certain you will be able to include in your report to the funder.

- Include a moving closing section to reinforce the key points in the proposal and repeat "the ask."

Sample Grant Proposal Narrative

The Ralph Goodson Literacy Project would like to request a $20,000 grant from the Jones Family Foundation to support its family literacy project, an essential component in its programs designed to break the cycle of poverty across generations.

Whether someone will graduate from high school is frequently determined by the age of three. A child's early experiences with books and stories, including how they associate them with the adults in their lives, strongly influence their development of language and literacy skills.

According to Love for Books and the Elementary Education Data Center, children who are struggling readers in first grade are 88% more likely to still be struggling in fourth grade, the second critical point in a child's education. The fourth grade is when children start to depend on reading to learn other subjects, which is why fourth graders who do not read on grade level are four times more likely to drop out of high school.

Some 39% of children under five years of age in our community live in poverty. They do not have an opportunity to gain the basic literacy skills needed to be on track by fourth grade and to serve them throughout their education. An additional roadblock to success for many of these children is the limited literacy of parents. Parent participation is crucial in developing a love and tradition of reading.

The Ralph Goodson Literacy Project works with children from age two through third grade to instill the basic literacy skills needed to provide a foundation for their entire education. We also work to increase literacy skills and confidence in parents so that they can take an active role in their children's education.

The Success of Our Approach

More than 85% of children who take part in at least one year of our program reach grade-level reading by the critical fourth grade benchmark. Past participants in our program are only now beginning to graduate from high school, but preliminary surveys indicate a 90% on-time graduation rate.

Parents and community leaders have recognized the Ralph Goodson Literacy Project for its stunning results. Mary R., a mother of three children in our program, tells us that, "The books given to our family by the Ralph Goodson Literacy Project completely changed my children's lives. I didn't grow up with books and always had a hard time in school. Staff members of the Project showed me how to create and hold our child's interest in reading, and I was so proud when she started first grade reading as well as children who attended private kindergartens."

The Literacy Project's work with children was recognized in 2015 by the Mayor's Office as one of three "Community Stars" for its work with children.

Long-term major support from the Community Foundation (ten years) and the Big City News (five years) also demonstrates the esteem in which the Literacy Project is held by leaders in the community. The Community

Foundation, however, recently informed us that its grants must end after this year due to its policy on the number of consecutive years funding is permitted, which is why we are seeking new support.

Our Programs

The Ralph Goodson Literacy Project works with young people and their families in the inner city to promote literacy and the pursuit of knowledge. We do this through three initiatives.

(1) <u>Early Years</u>: To develop a love of reading in the early years, we sponsor story times at daycare centers. Volunteers read to the two- to four-year-olds twice a week, leading to the children recognizing words and beginning to read. Art projects based on the stories extend the children's interests. Children can take home copies of the stories they have heard to share with their families.

(2) <u>Foundational Years</u>: We also work with children in grades K-3 to develop reading skills to further learning in all subjects. After-school tutoring ensures that each child will reach or exceed his grade-appropriate reading level. Students are encouraged to complete writing exercises about what they have read to develop skills and learn to express themselves in writing.

(3) <u>Family Literacy</u>: Reading skills must be cultivated at home to become engrained. Many parents, however, lack good reading skills. In these cases, volunteer tutors work with entire families on reading skills in one of our four centers, or, in some circumstances, make house calls for the more difficult-to-reach families.

We have found that this holistic approach provides the best environment over a sustained period to develop advanced reading skills in children.

Family Literacy

We are seeking your support specifically for the family literacy program, which seeks to improve reading and writing skills in families with multi-generational illiteracy. Ralph Goodson, our founder, was himself a child of illiterate parents, which is why he founded this organization. Because of the success of this initiative, it has remained our signature program.

Illiteracy too frequently becomes a tradition handed down from parents to their children. Many adults have learned to function well enough that few people, even those close to them, realize they are illiterate. Nonetheless, illiteracy holds them back and is the major contributor to the poverty in which these families inevitably live.

The Social Thinkers Forum's 2009 report on children with inadequate reading and writing skills found that "in the majority of cases studied, children's literacy problems stem from having illiterate or barely literate parents."

Getting to the families that can most benefit from this service requires a number of strategies because illiteracy is not something adults readily admit. The Ralph Goodson Literacy Project seeks to identify and address these families by:

<u>Working with schools</u>. We hold an orientation meeting for elementary school reading teachers and counselors twice each year to acquaint them with our programs. In addition, we help them understand the signs present when a child might have illiterate parents. By asking parents in for counseling sessions with a staff member from the school and from the Goodson Project, we can broach the topic of the parent's literacy through a private discussion of the problems their child is experiencing.

<u>Working with job training centers</u>. We meet regularly with counselors at the major job training sites throughout the county. These counselors are trained to work with illiterate adults, but we ask that they call us in when they discover the adults are parents. Adults are more comfortable approaching literacy training as another job skill rather than as a shortcoming.

<u>Working with employers</u>. Twelve of the county's largest employers of unskilled and low-skilled laborers work with us to offer literacy training as a job benefit. When adults see the clear relationship between job advancement and literacy, they are typically more willing to address this problem. We work with other literacy organizations so that we can concentrate our efforts on those employees with children and include methods they can use to work with their children.

Through these outreach efforts, we will identify families with multi-generational literacy problems. We anticipate bringing into the program more than 200 families, and we expect that at least 60% of them will continue in the program for the entire school year. Based on our eleven-year experience, of the families that participate for six months, 90 percent complete a full year in the program, and virtually all of those families will sign up the following year. Including families already in the program, we will work with at least 420 families during the grant period.

Goodson Project teachers will work with families in several ways:

- Sessions with the children alone to reinforce what they are taught in the classroom.

- Sessions with the parents to help them overcome any embarrassment they might feel in front of their children because of their lack of reading and writing skills.

- Sessions with parents and children in which they share their skills by reading aloud together and working on family writing and art projects.

The sessions with both parents and children are the key to the program's success. By making reading and writing family activities, the shared skills become an integral part of how family members relate to one another, thus strengthening both skills and family bonds.

Most family sessions are held at the Goodson Project's facilities, although teachers frequently make "house calls" to families for which transportation to downtown is a hardship or who cannot attend scheduled sessions because of their work hours.

One parent who participated in the program last year told us that, "Being able to read with my daughter has brought us closer than ever before." Another parent commented that, "My Sara is so bright that I have to stay up late studying to keep up with her, but it's worth it to see her doing so much better in school." The program equally affects the children. Billy, one of three children in a family, let us know that, "We all look forward to our weekly session with Ms. Thomas. The new books she brings us are great, and she even finds ones my dad wants to read."

The Family Literacy initiative is led by Muriel Spooner, who has worked in this program for twelve years, starting as a case worker and moving up to supervisor and, for the last five years, as program director. She is assisted by a core of fifteen staff members and ten volunteers, all of whom have education degrees. These teachers work directly with families. The partnerships with schools, job centers, and employers noted above provide administrative support for the program, as well as free program space.

Evaluation

Teachers conduct formative evaluations of students' progress through weekly reports submitted to the program director. This gives the director the ability to determine if any additional assistance is required and act immediately. She performs a summative evaluation at the end of the school year by compiling and synthesizing teachers' reports and combining them with school reports on the children's final grades. A short year-end survey of parents collects their impressions of the program and the teachers, supplying a rounded picture of the program.

We employ an outside evaluator to help us track students beyond their participation in the program. It can be difficult tracking a mobile population over the nine years between completing our program and high school graduation, but we are pleased that we so far have tracked as many as 75% of students through high school.

Present and Future Challenges

Overcoming the natural reluctance many adults feel in admitting to a lack of literacy skill will always be a challenge. Addressing literacy as a job skill has made the greatest inroads with this hard-to-reach group.

The extremely high teacher to client ratio of this program (1:7 per session) provides the dramatic results for which the program is known. This ratio, however, makes it an expensive program to run. We believe that, given the employment opportunities it creates for the present and the next generation as well as the contribution it makes toward more stable families, the program uses its fund efficiently.

We hope you will join the Ralph Goodson Literacy Project in improving literacy in our community through the Family Literacy initiative with a $20,000 grant. By acquiring literacy skills, the cycle of poverty can be broken, lives made richer, and children reach their full potential. On behalf of all our clients, we thank you again for your kind consideration of this request.

Please note that the Ralph Goodson Literacy Project is a fictional organization used here for illustration purposes.

Additional Sample Grants

At GrantSpace.org, created by the Foundation Center, you can find many resources, including a variety of real grants from a wide variety of nonprofits. See http://grantspace.org/tools/sample-documents.

About the Author

Waddy Thompson's thirty-three-year career in arts administration has encompassed work for a wide variety of organizations serving music, dance, theatre, literature, and visual arts. He has held positions at The Whitney Museum of American Art, InterSchool Orchestras of New York, New York Foundation for the Arts, Poets & Writers, OPERA American, Second Stage Theatre, Symphony Space, and the Authors Guild Foundation. His responsibilities at these organizations included fundraising, donor-advised funds, marketing, communications, and various administrative areas. He has secured donations, grants, and bequests up to one million dollars from the full spectrum of funding sources.

He is also the author of the *The Wise Guide to Winning Grants* (Stitch-in-Time Books, 2017), *The Complete Idiot's Guide to Grant Writing* (Alpha Books, 2014), and numerous articles in *The NonProfit Times* and other periodicals. He has taught grant writing for New York University's Heyman Center for Philanthropy and Fundraising and has also been a guest speaker and/or workshop presenter for several university programs and various arts councils and conferences.

Mr. Thompson is also a composer, and holds degrees from Eastman School of Music (B.M.) and Florida State University (M.M. and D.M.).

Author's Note

Dear Reader,

I hope you found this book helpful in writing grant proposals. If so, I invite you to review it on any of the online booksellers.

Thank you

This book is also available as an audiobook from Amazon.com, Audible.com, and iTunes.com

Also by Waddy Thompson:

The Wise Guide to Winning Grants (Stitch-in-Time Books, February 2017), a comprehensive guide to researching, writing, managing, and reporting on grants. Also includes information on freelance grant writing.

The *Quick* Wise Guide to Fundraising Readiness (Stitch-in-Time Books, January 2018), a guide for board members and executive staff about how to prepare to raise money, even before hiring fundraising staff or consultants.

You can find more information on fundraising at GrantAdviser.com

www.ingramcontent.com/pod-product-compliance
Lightning Source LLC
Chambersburg PA
CBHW052136010526
44113CB00036B/2286